Peeping in the Shell

A Whooping Crane Is Hatched

FAITH McNULTY

illustrations by Irene Brady

Harper & Row, Publishers

Library of Congress Cataloging-in-Publication Data
McNulty, Faith.
   Peeping in the shell.

   Summary: Describes how a scientist courts a whooping
crane and how the resulting egg is carefully incubated
until it hatches.
   1. Whooping cranes—Juvenile literature.   2. Whooping
cranes—Eggs—Juvenile literature.   3. Eggs—Incubation—
Juvenile literature.   4. Birds, Protection of—Juvenile
literature.   5. Birds—Eggs—Juvenile literature.
[1. Whooping cranes.   2. Eggs—Incubation.   3. Birds—
Protection]   I. Brady, Irene, ill.   II. Title.
QL696.G84M38 1986   639.9′7831   85-45837
ISBN 0-06-024134-9
ISBN 0-06-024135-7 (lib. bdg.)

To George Archibald
and The International Crane Foundation

PART I

Picture a big, white bird—the biggest bird you have ever seen. Picture it standing. Its body is balanced on long, thin legs. It holds its head high on a long, curved neck. A patch of red on top of its head looks like a tiny cap. There are spots of red on each cheek and a mask of black feathers. The bird's beak is long and sharp as a sword.

Suppose you stand close to the bird. If you are between four and five feet tall, the bird is as tall as you are. This is the tallest bird in North America.

Now suppose the bird sees an insect moving in the grass. It tilts its head and its lemon yellow eyes seem to flash as it spies its prey. Swiftly the long, sharp beak stabs at the earth. For an instant you might glimpse a wriggling grasshopper before the bird swallows it.

If there is water nearby—a marsh or pond—the bird might decide to fish. Minnows, crabs and other tiny water animals are its favorite foods. As the bird unfolds its wings to fly, black tips appear. The great wings measure seven feet from tip to tip—wider than the outstretched arms of a tall man.

Now the bird leans forward, runs a few steps and flaps into the air. It rises slowly, like a plane taking off. Its wings beat in short, strong strokes, lifting the heavy body. In the air it glides easily, now rising, now skimming the marsh grass, searching for the best place to land. As the bird nears the earth, it seems to hang in the air. Then, lowering its legs like landing gear, it gently alights at the water's edge.

With long, slow steps, the bird wades into the water. Its keen eyes scan the sandy bottom. Its long beak can plunge into the shallow water so swiftly that even a darting minnow or a skittering crab cannot escape.

Suddenly something startles the bird. Perhaps a heron or a gull dares fly too close. The great white bird raises its head and gives a bugle call. It is a strange, wild sound—something like the blast of a trumpet, something like a person whooping at the top of his lungs. It is this voice that gives the bird its name: whooping crane.

One hundred years ago there were a good many places in America where you might have seen whooping cranes. In winter you might have seen them in several southern states, near a marsh or at the shore.

In spring most of the whooping cranes flew north to nest. They once nested in marshes in the northern prairies, but that was a long time ago. The marshes have since been drained and turned into plowed fields. Cities, towns and farms have taken over all the places in the United States where whooping cranes once nested. Now they nest only in a small area in Canada.

It is in a dense wilderness called Wood Buffalo State Park. There is no road to it. In recent years a few people have reached the crane's nesting ground by airplane—not to harm the cranes, but to help them survive.

In the United States today you can see wild whooping cranes at their winter refuge on the Texas Coast, near the town of Aransas. Usually about fifty whooping cranes spend the winter there. In good years there are a few more; in bad years, less. They are the only wild whooping cranes left on earth. This is a very small number, and whooping cranes are on the list of species that might become extinct.

At the Aransas Refuge the whooping cranes do not stay in a flock, but spread out along the shore in family groups. A pair of cranes usually raises only one chick each season. If you visited the refuge you would probably see pairs with young cranes that were hatched in Canada the summer before. The young are a rusty pink color that changes to white as they grow up. During the winter the parent cranes feed their young one and also teach it to find its own food.

In spring the cranes gather in small groups and take to the air. They circle higher and higher, then begin the long, long flight to their nesting place in Canada—twenty-two hundred miles away.

About thirty-five years ago conservationists—people who care about wildlife—realized that little by little whooping cranes were decreasing in number. Many cranes had been shot by hunters. Each year the cranes found fewer safe places to nest and raise their young. The wild shores and marshes where whooping cranes spent the winter were no longer wild and safe for them.

Year after year more cranes died than were hatched, or than lived to grow up and start new families. For some years no one noticed or cared that few whooping cranes could be seen where once there had been many. When people did notice—and care—it was almost too late to save the cranes. At this time, in the 1930s, there were only twenty or thirty whooping cranes left on earth. Unless they were protected quickly, there would soon be none at all.

It is lucky for the whooping cranes—and for all of us who love wildlife—that some people *did* care about the cranes. Our government's Fish and Wildlife Service bought the land at Aransas and turned it into a refuge—safe from hunters.

Then, about twenty years ago, the service began to

raise whooping cranes in captivity with the hope that their children or grandchildren could someday be set free. The first step was to take eggs from wild whooping cranes.

Whooping cranes nest on the ground in marshy areas. Their large nests made of sticks and grasses, and the big white birds themselves, are easy to spot from the air. Each summer biologists flew to the nesting grounds and stole a few eggs. To make sure the chicks inside would not be harmed, the eggs were put in special boxes padded with foam rubber and warmed by heaters. The eggs were taken early in the season, allowing the mother cranes time to lay a second egg to replace the lost one and raise the chick before autumn came. Thus, stealing the eggs did no harm to the wild cranes.

The stolen eggs were flown to the Fish and Wildlife Research Center at Patuxent, Maryland, and put in

incubators—special devices for hatching eggs. The word incubate comes from a Latin word meaning "to lie on." Mother birds sit on their eggs, keeping them warm and safe while the chick inside grows from a tiny speck called an embryo to a baby bird ready to enter the world. However, if an egg is put in a box, kept at the right temperature, and is turned over at intervals—the way a mother bird turns her eggs with her beak—the embryo will develop as well as if a mother bird were caring for it herself. In this way at least a hundred whooping crane eggs have been hatched at Patuxent. Now scientists are experimenting to find the best way to set these cranes free.

PART II

Now we come to the strange story of Tex and George. Tex is a whooping crane. George Archibald is a man who has loved birds since he was a small boy. At college he studied ornithology, as the study of birds is called. He became particularly interested in the crane family and decided to spend his life working for their welfare.

Whooping cranes have relatives in Asia, Africa, Russia and Australia. Like whooping cranes, many other species of cranes are in danger of dying out unless the people of the countries in which they live decide to help them survive. Ten years ago, after graduating from college, George and a friend, Ron Sauey, started a center for breeding all kinds of cranes. Ron Sauey's father gave them the use of a farm he owned in

Baraboo, Wisconsin, where George and Ron set up The Crane Center.

George and Ron traveled to far parts of the world and brought the eggs of many kinds of rare cranes back to Baraboo. Once, when George was in an airplane, carefully holding the egg of a rare Siberian crane in his lap, it began to hatch. By the time he landed he was holding not an egg, but a tiny, newborn chick.

Tex, the whooping crane, was hatched in a zoo. Her parents were wild cranes captured some years before. Tex was a small, weak chick, and the zoo director feared that without special attention she might die. He put her in a box in his kitchen and fed and cared for her himself.

All baby birds become attached to the human or animal they first see. Normally this would be their own parents. But if a human feeds and cares for a baby bird, it will behave as though the person were its mother. This is called imprinting, and it can have strange results. For instance, there was the case of an orphan duckling that a farmer raised in a pen along with a dog. The duckling became imprinted by the dog. She followed it everywhere, and even as a grown duck liked dogs better than ducks. Perhaps the duck thought she was a dog. No one can tell just what happens in the mind of an animal.

Something like this happened in the case of Tex. When she grew up, she liked humans better than whooping cranes. When she was put with a male crane, she fought him and refused to mate. For many years it seemed that Tex would never be a mother. When George Archibald heard about Tex and her lonely life, he decided to see what he could do to change it. Because whooping cranes are so rare, he felt that no chance to get Tex to lay eggs should be wasted.

George brought Tex to The Crane Center at Baraboo.

He put her in a little house of her own with a grassy yard and set about making friends with her. George believed that Tex thought she was a human and that what she wanted was a human mate. He decided to do everything he could to play the part.

George put a cot in Tex's house and slept there every night for weeks. He talked to her. Tex began to answer with crane noises—the sort of sounds that whooping cranes utter when they "talk" to their mates. Whooping cranes become very attached to their mates. If one of a pair is injured or dies, the other will stay by its side for a long time. Their feelings may not be like human love, but in some ways seem to resemble it.

Wild whooping cranes mate in spring. Before mating they spend a time in courtship. The male pays close attention to the female. Several times a day the pair do what has been called a "dance." They leap into the air, whirl about and bow to each other. They spread their

great white wings, showing the black tips, and flutter them like fans. They bounce up and down as though their long legs were pogo sticks. They become very excited and seem to enjoy themselves, as human dancers do.

During courtship, changes take place in the female's body, and she becomes ready to mate. For wild cranes, mating is simple enough. The female crouches on the ground and raises her tail feathers. The male gets on her back and presses his penis (yes, male birds have a small penis inside their vent) against her opening (in birds this is called a cloaca) and transfers semen to fertilize the egg that has formed inside her.

By the time spring came, Tex had begun to behave as though George were her natural mate. Now it was time for him to court her. He moved her to a large, open meadow, where she would have room to roam as though she were free. Tex had a crippled wing, so there was no chance she would fly away. George built a small shelter for himself.

Then what many people might call the world's strangest courtship began.

All through the day George gave Tex his full attention. He walked with her as she searched the grass for insects. He helped her gather hay and sticks, and pile them together to make a nest. When she lay down to rest, George stayed by her side.

From time to time George danced with Tex. It isn't easy for a man to dance like a crane. George flapped his arms, whirled and leaped until he was breathless. Soon Tex joined him in the dance, and George began to hope that his plan was succeeding and that Tex would become ready to form an egg.

One day, while Tex was resting, George wrote to a friend: "Tex and I began our courtship April 1, and it goes on from dawn to dusk. In spite of a few wet days, it

has been a lovely April with wild swans and wood ducks flying over and adding a touch of the wild to the hayfield where Tex and I have our territory. I have a card table in my shed, a bench and a folding chair where I can read and write. Outside my open door, Tex stands preening by her bucket of water and dish of pellets. Every few hours she straightens into an upright, alert posture. Then with beak slightly raised, she makes a low 'purr...r...r' call. It is a sign that she wants me to go somewhere with her. Usually it is just an intruder (a crow or a jay) that she warns off with a trumpet call. Sometimes she wants to dance in the shorter grass just up the hill. At the end of the dance, when she has had enough of leaping, whirling and bowing, she struts with her tail lifted—a sign that she is getting ready to mate. When I stroke her back gently, she is satisfied and begins to preen her feathers.

"At such times she forgets about me, and I have a

chance to run up the hill to the office to do other things. These moments, and the time after dark when I sneak away for a night's sleep in my own bed, are the only times I leave Tex. By April 10 her cloaca was enlarged to the point that I knew we must begin artificial insemination."

Artificial insemination is often done in breeding domestic animals and birds when it is not possible to bring the male and female together. Semen from a male can be collected in a bottle, kept frozen until needed and then put into the female with a syringe. To inseminate Tex, George arranged to have frozen semen from a male whooping crane at the Patuxent research center shipped to him at Baraboo.

When Tex's behavior showed that an egg had formed in her ovary and was ready to be fertilized, George prepared himself with a syringe of semen. He danced with her, and when, at the end of the dance, she crouched down, he stroked her back and squirted the semen into her cloaca with the syringe. This was done several times.

Then a period of anxious waiting began. George stayed on with Tex, praying that an egg had been fertilized and was developing inside her. He knew this could take several weeks.

Though George watched Tex closely, he could see no change to give him a clue that insemination had succeeded. Then suddenly on May 1, she behaved very differently.

That morning Tex seemed weak. It took her an hour to stroll slowly up the hill to the center of the hayfield. She did not dance, or call to George, or strut or flutter her wings as she usually did every day. George worried that she might be ill. On the other hand her unusual quietness might mean that an egg had formed and was moving down into her lower abdomen. George noticed that Tex ate only a quarter of her normal diet of pellets. This was a good sign. George knew that for a few days before laying an egg, cranes eat very little. Perhaps this is to leave room inside the abdomen for the egg to move down to the cloaca.

By late afternoon Tex had perked up a bit. In the evening she and George enjoyed a short dance in the fading light. At the end of it, George stroked her back and ran his fingers over Tex's abdomen, hoping to feel a lump—the egg. He felt nothing unusual, but he could see that her cloaca was swollen. With a thrill of excitement he decided an egg was on the way.

That night George did not go home to bed but took his sleeping bag to the meadow and slept beside Tex under the stars. In the morning Tex was unchanged, but she began to arrange the straw they had gathered into a nest. The spot she chose was near her water bucket. George stayed with her again that night, stretched out beside Tex, who slept standing on one leg.

At five in the morning George was awakened by Tex calling her low, purring call. She wanted to dance. Sleepily George got up and they danced in the dim light of dawn. Again he felt her abdomen. No egg. His spirits sank. A short while later his hopes rose again when Tex went back to work, building a nest.

This was Sunday. George decided to slip away for an hour to go to church. He is a devout man and he prayed for Tex—and for a new whooping crane. When he returned he found Tex waiting beside his sleeping bag. She ran eagerly to meet him. They danced, and at the end of the dance he felt her abdomen.

"I could feel a lump," George wrote in a letter to a friend. "It was hard and rounded. I knew it must be an egg, still deep within her warm body, but destined for the skies!"

23

All that morning Tex gave no sign that she was about to lay, until shortly after noon when she began to call out. With her head lowered over the nesting spot she gave out loud, hoarse cries. George had never heard her make such sounds before.

A little later she sat down on the nest and, reaching out with her long beak, pulled the nesting hay close around her. Her cries continued for an hour. Then she stopped calling, and with a half-opened beak, began to pant.

George watched with anxiety as she seemed to struggle to push out the egg. There was no way he could help. As Tex's effort increased, she stretched out flat on the nest so that her neck lay in a curve on the ground. At last George, kneeling beside her, saw the egg appear. It was greenish, with brown speckles, and about three times the size of a hen's egg. To George it was a miraculous sight. He felt a tremendous thrill—a combination of relief that his plan had succeeded, and hope that within the egg lay the promise of adding one more whooping crane to the small number on earth.

PART III

Since this story is true, it is time to explain how it came to be told. I—the person writing these words—am a woman who studies and writes about birds and animals. I have been to the whooping cranes' refuge in Texas and seen them fly over the marshes like great white gliders.

I've seen whooping cranes standing tall and proud on the shore and marching royally along the beach. I think they are wonderful birds.

I live in New England, far from the home of Tex and George in Baraboo, but when I read about George's work to save all kinds of cranes, I became greatly interested. We met and became friends. This was before his experiment with Tex. He told me of his plan. He said he knew some people would make fun of him, and that it might sound silly for a man to try to behave like a whooping crane, but that he didn't care. He said he would do whatever was needed to bring another whooping crane into the world.

Sitting in his shed in the hayfield with Tex, George wrote me a long letter telling me how the egg had been laid. Then, one morning in June, I answered my telephone and heard George's voice. He sounded joyful.

"It's peeping in the shell!" he said. "We can hear the chick! It will hatch today or tomorrow. Please come out and see it happen."

I answered that I couldn't come so far on such short notice. I wished him luck and said good-bye. But I couldn't stop thinking about George and the egg. I wondered what there would be to see when the egg hatched. I supposed I would simply see an egg, like the one I'd had for breakfast, only bigger. I supposed hatching meant that the chick would break the shell and step out. None of that sounded very exciting.

Then I thought about whooping cranes: how marvelous it is that there are any at all; how marvelous that George Archibald, and many other people, are trying so hard to keep these great birds flying.

I thought about Tex: her strange life story and what seemed to be her idea that she was a human rather than a bird. Suddenly I wanted very much to see her chick come into the world. I telephoned George and told him I would take the next plane to Baraboo.

Late that afternoon I arrived at The Crane Center in Baraboo. It is on a hill surrounded by rolling fields.

George met me, smiling. He is a slim man in his thirties, with reddish, curly hair, wide brown eyes, and a gentle, almost shy manner.

George told me the egg was in an incubator. He explained that many of the eggs of the rare cranes at the center are taken from the nest and hatched in incubators for two reasons: one, it is safer for the egg because parent cranes may accidentally break an egg; two, if her first egg is taken away, a female bird will usually lay a second. In that way twice as many chicks can be hatched each year.

George led me into the building. We walked past old horse stalls and went downstairs to a basement room. In one corner was a large wooden box about the size of a chest of drawers. It had two doors, each with a small window. George went to the window on the right, bent down, switched on a light inside and peered through the glass.

29

"There it is," he said proudly. "Isn't it beautiful!" He moved over so I could look in.

The floor of the incubator was level with my eyes. In the center lay the egg—about five inches long and greenish with brown speckles. The floor on which it lay was covered with green plastic carpet. Two scraps of foam rubber cradled the egg. Its round end faced us. The egg lay as still as a stone in a museum case. The shell hid the secret of whatever might be inside.

I remembered I once had an Easter egg with a window at one end. I told George I wished this egg had a window. He pointed out something I had missed. At the end of the egg facing us, small cracks covered an area the size of a dime. In the center was a tiny hole. George said this was the first stage of hatching. The chick had hammered at the shell with its beak, making the crack and the tiny hole. George called this first breakthrough pipping.

30

A tall, dark-haired young man wearing a denim shirt and jeans joined us. He was Mike Putnam. Mike is an aviculturist—that is, he has special training in breeding birds. Like the doctor at the birth of a human baby, Mike would be in charge of the hatching of the whooping crane.

Mike took a turn looking in the window. I noticed a low humming sound coming from the incubator. George said that it came from a fan inside that kept warm, moist air moving around the egg.

"Let's see how the chick sounds," George suggested.

Mike opened the incubator door. He leaned close to the egg and made a low crooning sound.

"He's making the sounds a mother crane makes," George explained.

Then Mike spoke to the egg. "Hello, there!" he said softly. "How're you doing?" He cocked his head to listen, and a smile spread over his face. "Good!" he exclaimed.

31

"Real good! He's peeping just fine," he told George.

Mike moved over and George leaned close to the egg. Then he, too, smiled a wide smile and offered me a turn. I bent down and heard a tiny voice whispering inside the egg.

Mike closed the door of the incubator and we three sat down on straight chairs and talked. I asked how long it would take for the chick to hatch.

"Each chick is different," Mike said. "A strong chick may peck its way out in twelve hours. Some chicks take as long as thirty-six hours—a day and a half. If a chick does not succeed in getting out in that time, it is in danger of dying in the shell."

"This is a funny egg," George said. "It's a little lop-sided and wrinkled at one end. It's been giving me fits."

George explained that a whooping crane chick is usually ready to hatch about twenty-eight days after the egg is laid. For the last twenty-eight days, George said, he had worried constantly about this egg. He told of the dangers the egg had survived.

Soon after Tex laid the egg, George picked it up carefully and carried it to the nest of a pair of sandhill cranes that are experienced parents. He thought it would be safer in their care than if he left it with Tex, who had never hatched an egg. He gave Tex a dummy egg, and she was happy sitting on it.

Every few days George and Mike checked the egg. They carried a tiny scale to the nest, picked up the egg and weighed it. They soon found it was losing weight too rapidly. This was a bad sign. It meant that the liquid inside the egg was somehow coming out through the shell. Perhaps the shell was thinner than it should be, or too porous. An eggshell has tiny pores like the pores in skin. If they are too large, liquid inside the egg evaporates and the growing chick dries out and dies.

Hoping to stop this drying out, George put a plastic swimming pool in the pen with the foster parents. He thought that if they got their breast feathers wet and then sat on the egg, this moisture might keep the egg from drying out. It didn't work. The egg continued to lose weight.

Now George tried pouring water over the egg every few hours. Still the egg lost weight. George was more worried each day. When the egg was eighteen days old, George took it from the nest and put it in an incubator. The humidity was turned up high, filling the air around the egg with moisture. This was no help either. The egg was still losing weight twice as fast as a normal egg.

George thought of trying to inject water into the egg with a hypodermic needle. He telephoned experts at the Patuxent research center. They advised him not to do it. "Too dangerous," they said.

George then telephoned Dr. Bernard Wentworth, an expert at the University of Wisconsin. Dr. Wentworth had a better idea of how to get water into the shell.

He hurried to Baraboo, carrying a portable icebox. Inside was a jar filled with sterilized ice water. He gently put the egg into the icy water and kept it there for five minutes. The cold caused the chick and the rest of the contents of the egg to shrink, making an empty space inside the egg. This empty space drew water into the egg through the pores of the shell.

The egg was given this treatment once a day for several days. From then on, when George and Mike weighed the egg, its weight loss was normal.

Every once in a while during our talk, George or Mike would get up and take a look at the egg. Nothing was happening. There were no more cracks than before. The tiny hole was no larger. Mike said the chick must be resting.

By now it was supper time. We were all tired and hungry. George and Mike talked over the question of who should sit up all night to watch the egg. Two young women who were assistants at The Crane Center came in to see the wonderful egg. They offered to spend the night with it. They would bring sleeping bags and take turns watching. If anything happened they would call Mike.

George and Mike and I said good-night to the egg and went out to dinner.

PART IV

At nine o'clock the next morning, I went back to the incubator room. I found Mike there. He told me George had been suddenly called away by an important problem. This left Mike in sole charge of the egg.

Mike said the egg had spent a quiet night—too quiet. He was disappointed that it had not made more progress. I peered in the window and saw that a few bits of shell had been chipped away. The tiny hole had become a slot about a quarter of an inch long. I could faintly see something quivering in the darkness in the depths of the shell.

For the next hour I sat beside the incubator. From

time to time I looked in at the egg. Sometimes I saw something moving beneath the slot, but mostly the chick was quiet.

Mike sat at a table beside me, making notes in a large ledger. Across the room two incubators of another type made a low humming noise. I asked Mike about them. He explained that they held the crop of eggs laid this spring by other species of cranes—about forty eggs in all.

He pulled open a drawer in the incubator. Large, speckled eggs lay in rows on trays. In this kind of incubator the trays are slowly moved by a revolving drum so that from time to time the eggs are gently turned over—a job that mother cranes do by nudging them over with their beaks.

Mike took a tray of eggs out of the incubator and put it on the table in front of him. He began to pick up eggs, one by one, and make notes in his ledger.

eggs over easy!

As I watched I noticed a poster on the wall above the table. Printed on it in large type was a list:

Eggstatic	Eggsplain
Eggspensive	Eggspect
Eggshausted	Eggsotic
Eggseptional	Eggsistential
Eggsposed	Eggsellent
Eggstra	Eggsorbitant
Eggspert	Eggs Over Easy

Action! I glanced into the incubator and saw that a bit of shell had fallen from the rim of the hole in the egg. The tip of a beak stuck out, wavered and fell back. I called Mike. He got up and opened the door. "Hi, there!" he called in a crooning voice. A series of tiny, piping cries answered. The sound was eager and urgent, but very, very, small. For an instant the beak thrust out of the hole.

"You're doing real good," Mike said encouragingly,

and shut the door. The beak continued to poke out, nod and disappear, as though the chick were trying to reach out to us.

"How much longer will it take to hatch?" I asked.

"Lots longer," Mike replied. He went back to work on the eggs in the tray before him. He picked up an egg, held it up to a light bulb and with a pencil drew a slanting line on the shell.

As he worked, he explained that a chick forms inside a sac which does not quite fill the egg, leaving an airspace at one end. By looking at an egg against a bright light, he was able to see the dark form of the chick within the sac and the paler outline of the airspace. The slanting pencil line was to mark their position—something that would be important to know later, when the egg began to hatch.

I asked Mike to tell me about the stages an egg goes through before a chick hatches. They are more complicated and filled with danger than I had imagined.

While a chick develops, it needs oxygen and food. It gets them through a cord attached to a yolk which is in turn attached to a membrane lining the shell of the egg. The membrane has blood cells that draw oxygen from the outside air through the pores of the shell. The yolk contains a store of food to nourish the growing embryo.

When the chick is fully formed and ready to hatch, it begins to scratch at the sac that holds it. When the sac tears, the chick thrusts its head into the airspace and begins to breathe. At this point the egg must be right side up, otherwise the fluid that has surrounded the chick in the sac may drain into the airspace and drown the chick. Mike explained that he had outlined the airspace on each egg so that when hatching time came, he could be sure the chick was in proper position.

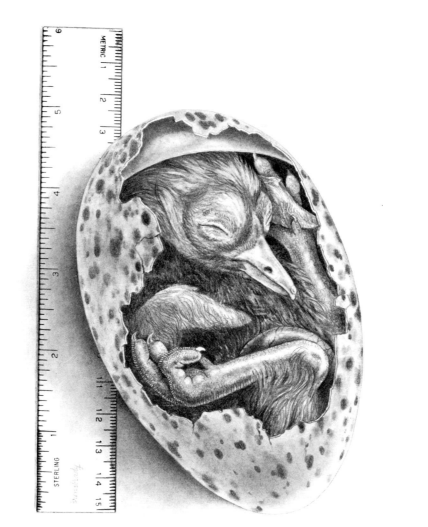

After the sac is torn, a series of miraculous changes begins. As the chick begins to breathe air into its lungs, the blood vessels in the membrane are no longer needed. They begin to wither. At this stage the chick is like a diver depending on an air tank. The air supply inside the egg is limited, and the chick must reach the outer air by making a hole in the shell before the oxygen in the airspace is used up.

As the chick begins to breathe, it utters its first peeps and its mother answers. The sound of her voice encourages the chick to continue to peck at the shell. Our chick has passed these stages—scratching, peeping and pipping—but it still has much work to do to free itself.

Within the next few hours the chick should peck a line of holes circling the end of the egg. When the circle is complete, the end of the shell can be pushed off, setting the chick free. To peck a ring of holes the chick must turn inside the egg. Mike calls this spinning. It had been almost a day since our chick pipped. By now it should have begun to spin.

For two more hours I sat by the incubator, looking in now and then. From time to time the chick pecked at the edges of the slot. Sometimes I saw its beak stick out of the slot, wave back and forth, and then sink back as though the chick were too tired to go on trying. Then it would be quiet for a while.

At intervals Mike got up, opened the door and talked to the chick. Each time I could see its beak poke out in response, wave frantically, then disappear. I was beginning to feel anxious.

"Is he spinning?" I asked Mike as he shut the door.

"Not yet," Mike said. "Give him time. It takes an awful lot of energy to hatch."

Two more hours went by, but the slot in the egg had not grown much bigger. Though the chick pecked, it wasn't able to crack the tough shell. If the end of the egg were the face of a clock, the chick had chipped away no more than the space between twelve and one. I began to feel that the chick was in trouble, and to wish Mike would do something.

After what seemed a long time, Mike opened the door again. He was greeted with frantic peeping—like cries for help.

"Hi, kid!" Mike said softly. "What's going on?" He picked up the egg and cradled it in his left hand. He gazed at it thoughtfully.

"I guess it's time to take a look," he said. "Maybe this guy isn't able to spin. Maybe something is holding him up."

With his right hand Mike picked up a pair of blunt scissors and gently nibbled at the edges of the hole, pulling away tiny bits of shell. The chick trilled excitedly. Suddenly I was able to see it—a dark shade

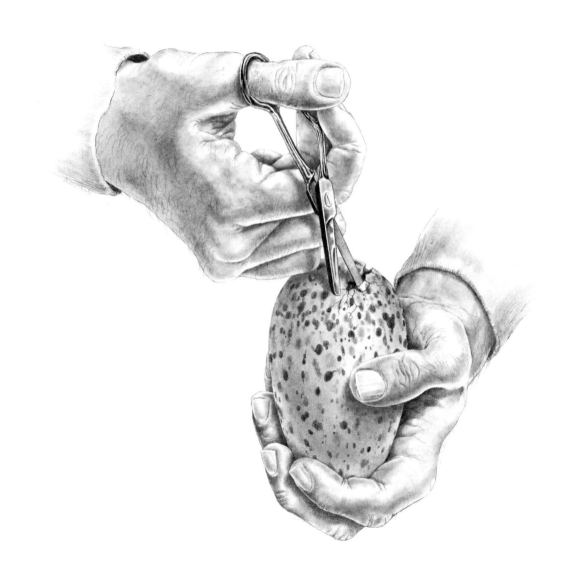

of pinkish brown, wet and leathery. I could see toes and a beak and the quills of one wing all cramped together.

Mike gently shoved the chick to one side with the scissors.

"Let's look at your membranes," he murmured, peering into the depths of the shell. He picked up a syringe and squirted a bit of liquid into the egg. Then he put the egg back in its foam rubber cradle on the green carpet and shut the door. For a few moments I could hear the chick's voice as it continued to peep. Then silence.

Mike explained that he had squirted water into the shell to wet the membranes in case they were stuck to the chick. He thought that might be the reason the chick wasn't spinning.

I asked Mike why he didn't simply pull the chick out of the shell.

Because, Mike explained, pulling it out suddenly

might kill it. During hatching, he went on, each step must take place at the proper time. While the chick is doing its work of pecking at the shell, the blood vessels that formerly supplied oxygen are drying up. If the chick were pulled out of the shell before these vessels had sealed themselves off, the chick might bleed to death.

Also, Mike went on, there is the yolk—a mass of concentrated food—that is pressed against the chick's underside near the tail. In another of the miraculous changes of hatching, this yolk is sucked into the chick's body through its umbilical cord. After the chick hatches, the yolk provides food for a day or so until the chick is strong enough to eat. The yolk should be inside the chick, and the umbilical cord dried up before the chick leaves the shell. Mike had seen that quite a bit of yolk had not yet been absorbed.

On the other hand, Mike explained, there is also

danger if hatching takes too long. While the chick is cramped inside the shell, it cannot breathe deeply because there is not enough room for its lungs to expand fully. After a time, a shortage of oxygen combined with exhaustion can cause the chick to give up and slowly die.

I looked at our poor egg and its bravely struggling prisoner with new anxiety. The chick seemed so frail, its task so tremendous.

Three hours later there had still been no change. The chick was resting. Or was it giving up? Mike had finished checking the trays of eggs and sat quietly reading a book. I wondered how he could be so calm. Later he told me that he had been as worried as I was, but didn't want to show it.

PART V

By mid-afternoon I was feeling not only anxious but also weary. I was tired of the windowless basement room, the straight chair, the humming sound of the incubators and the endless wait. I watched the chick as it quivered, struggled and rested again and again. It didn't seem to be getting anywhere.

Mike went on reading. I sensed that he didn't want to talk about the sad possibility that the chick might die. But I had to know what he thought.

"Mike," I asked, "is this hatching still normal? I mean, hasn't it taken too long?"

Mike looked up briefly. "It's getting close," he said, and went back to reading.

At the end of the next hour there had been quite a bit of change. The chick was peeping steadily. One leathery wing was exposed, pulsing with each peep. I could see the chick's fragile skull. It was thinly covered with wet feathers, like fine hair. The chick struggled steadily. Its beak waved and waved.

Mike put down his book. He got up and stared into the incubator for a long time. Then he picked up a forceps—a metal tool that resembles a pair of blunt scissors. He opened the door and placed the egg and its peeping occupant in his left hand. The motion excited the chick. It tried to raise its head, but its long neck sagged like limp spaghetti until its head rested on Mike's palm.

In this position the chick peeped more loudly than ever. It seemed to sense that a big moment was at hand. With great care Mike worked on the shell, removing large sections. Using the forceps to push the chick aside, he peered into the bottom of the shell.

"The membranes look good," he remarked, "but there is still quite a bit of yolk. He needs more time." He put

the egg back in its cradle and shut the door.

Mike sat down and picked up his book. Feeling a bit better, I sat down, too. Sometimes I watched the chick, sometimes the big clock on the wall.

By five o'clock there had been still more change. Now that half the shell was gone, the chick had been able to get the claws of one foot around the edge of the shell. It seemed to be trying to push itself out. One wing was clear. The head and neck were also totally free. At times the chick would lift its head on the long, frail neck. Then the neck would collapse, and the head sink onto the green carpet.

Mike had stopped reading. He sat beside me, watching intently. "One big push might do it," he remarked.

Several young men and women in jeans and tee shirts—the staff that cares for the other cranes—came into the room, hoping to see the big moment of hatching. The small basement room was crowded. The watchers talked in excited whispers as though they were in a human sick room.

With all eyes on him, Mike again lifted out the egg. The bird struggled and peeped. Its head wavered, then rested on Mike's palm. Mike was looking into the depths of the shell.

Looking over Mike's shoulder, I could see the glint of moisture and patches of blood at the bottom of the shell. Using the syringe, Mike dribbled in a few drops of water. He explained that it also contained a medicine to shrink the blood vessels and stop any bleeding. He put the egg back in the incubator. Now the chick, looking exhausted, lay half in and half out of the shell. Mike picked up a roll of white sticky tape and made two shoulder straps that held the bird in the shell. The chick looked as though it were wearing overalls.

"There is still too much blood and yolk," Mike explained. "I want to give him more time before he comes out."

There was a murmur of disappointment from the people watching. They began to drift away. A pretty blonde girl named Shirley asked me if I would like to go out to supper. It had been a long day. I had spent eight hours in that stuffy room, and I was hungry. But I didn't want to miss anything.

"What do you think?" I asked Mike.

"Go ahead," Mike said. "This little guy isn't going anywhere right now."

Two hours later I went back to the incubator room. I found Mike peering into the incubator, and he was smiling.

"Look!" he said. "He's out and he's okay."

There was the chick, lying on its breast, free at last. The empty shell had been removed. The chick's head nodded in groggy triumph as it tried to get up. The down covering its body was turning from brownish to pinkish yellow as it dried out.

"He just popped out a few minutes ago!" Mike said. "He gave a big push and busted loose. Doesn't he look great!" Mike was beaming with relief and joy.

The chick raised its head and I heard a tiny, piping whistle. It seemed to say, "I am here! I am a whooping crane, and it's great to be alive!"

THE EMPIRE
OF GHANA

The Empire of Ghana was also known as the Land of Gold.

~African Civilizations~

THE EMPIRE
OF GHANA

Rebecca L. Green

A First Book

Franklin Watts
A Division of Grolier Publishing
New York / London / Hong Kong / Sydney
Danbury, Connecticut

Photographs copyright ©: Trip/W Jacobs/Viesti Associates, Inc.: pp. 7, 46,
52; Alex de Sherbanin: p. 9; Werner Forman Archive/Art Resource, NY,
Courtesy Entwistle Gallery, London: p. 10; Paul Almasy/Corbis: p. 13;
Jonathan Blair/Corbis: p. 15; Yves Bresson/Gamma Liaison: p. 16; Nik
Wheeler/Corbis: pp. 19, 36; Trip/D Tunnicliffe/The Viesti Collection, Inc.:
p. 21; Aldo Tutino/Art Resource, NY: p. 22; M. Ascani/Liaison Interna-
tional: p. 23; Antony Bertin/Gamma Liaison: p.25; Congo Eric/Gamma
Liaison: p. 27; Werner Forman/Corbis: p.28; Gilles Coulon/Gamma
Liaison: p. 31; Serge Robert: pp. 32, 37; Trip/A Dalton/Viesti Associates,
Inc.: p. 33; Wolfgang Kaehler/Corbis: p. 39; Courtesy of Bernard de
Grunne: p. 41; Trip/M Jelliffe/Viesti Associates, Inc.: p. 45; Werner Forman
Archive/Art Resource, NY: pp. 48, 56; Trip/Trip/Viesti Associates, Inc.:
p. 49; The Purcell Team/Corbis: p. 54; Art Resource, NY: p. 58.

Library of Congress Cataloging-in-Publication Data

Green, Rebecca L.
    The empire of Ghana / Rebecca L. Green. — 1st ed.
      p.   cm. — (A first book)   (African civilizations)
    Includes bibliographical references and index.
    Summary: A survey of the history and culture of the West African
Empire of Ghana that, flourishing from about 750 until 1076, is not
related to modern Ghana.
    ISBN 0-531-20276-3
    1. Ghana (Empire)—History—Juvenile literature.   [1. Ghana
(Empire)—History.]   I. Title.   II. Series.   III. Series: African
civilizations.
DT532.15.G74   1998
966.1'016—dc21   97-37574
                                                               CIP
                                                                AC

Copyright © 1998 by The Rosen Publishing Group, Inc.
All rights reserved. Published simultaneously in Canada
Printed in the United States of America
1 2 3 4 5 6 7 8 9 10 R 05 04 03 02 01 00 99 98

CONTENTS

INTRODUCTION

The Empire of Ghana was the first great kingdom in West Africa. It is not related to the modern African country of Ghana, which in 1957 adopted the name of the ancient empire. The modern country of Ghana is located on the coast, bordering the Atlantic Ocean. The ancient Empire of Ghana, however, lay farther north in the region known as the Western Sudan.

The Western Sudan is in the interior of West Africa, far from the ocean. The kingdom was located just south of the great Sahara Desert, between the Niger River and the Senegal River in a region called Wangara. This area lies in the countries now called

A side stream of the Niger River runs through the Western Sudan. The dry savanna belt, known as the Sahel, dominates the Western Sudan.

Mali, Mauritania, and Senegal.

It is not known when ancient Ghana was founded, although it may have been as early as A.D. 250. We do know that it developed into a wealthy empire that flourished from about 750 until 1076. The remains of the ancient capital city, called Kumbi or Kumbi Saleh, were discovered in 1914 in Mauritania.

THE SONINKE

THE PEOPLE

Many different peoples lived in ancient Ghana. The earliest rulers may have come from the north or east. Most of ancient Ghana's inhabitants and rulers, however, were Mande-speaking Soninke people. They lived in an empire known for its incredible wealth, organization, and power. It is also famous for its rich culture and several centers of learning. Although their empire ended hundreds of years ago, the Soninke still live throughout the Western Sudan.

THE ORIGIN MYTH

Many cultures depend on oral histories instead of written books to remember the past. In West

Soninke man on horseback. The Soninke people were the founders of ancient Ghana.

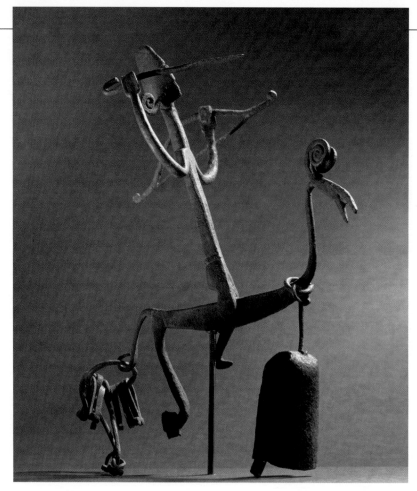

Iron, and the blacksmiths who worked it, played an important role in the early growth of ancient Ghana. This sculpture of a mounted archer was made by a blacksmith who lives in a region that was strongly influenced by the Empire of Ghana.

Africa, oral histories are studied and constantly retold by professional historians called *griots* (GREE-ohs). The oral histories about the origin of the Empire of Ghana begin with a story of the first Soninke ancestor, Dinga.

Dinga came from somewhere in the east and traveled a long time to reach the place that would become ancient Ghana. During his travels, Dinga stopped many times. He married many women and had many children with them.

When Dinga and his family finally settled, they established a group of small communities, each headed by one of Dinga's sons. These communities soon prospered and over time grew into the first powerful kingdom of the ancient Soninke.

The Soninke people were divided into *clans*. A clan is a group of families that all descend from one common ancestor. Each clan had a different name and performed a different job. For example, the Kante clan were blacksmiths and metalworkers, and the royal family were all from the Sisse clan.

THE STATE

The Soninke people who lived in ancient Ghana called themselves the Wago people. The word *wago* is still used today to describe the upper-class Soninke, people who are the descendants of Dinga and his sons.

The Wago people called their kingdom Wagadu. It was only later that Wagadu came to be known by the name Ghana, which is the Mande word for "war chief." When the kingdom of Wagadu was still young, the term *ghana* was used to describe its kings, but not the empire. Later, when Arabic writers wrote about the kingdom, they called it Biland Ghana, which means "the country (*biland*) of the king (*ghana*)" of the Soninke people. Eventually the phrase was shortened to Ghana, which came to mean the country of Wagadu instead of the king.

The term *ghana* emphasizes one of the king's important roles—military leader. The Soninke had a particularly fearsome military force because of their skill in working iron. They were probably the first people in the region to have iron technology— and for many years they were the only ones with this knowledge. Because they knew how to forge iron, they were able to make new and more powerful tools and weapons.

Metal tools made farming more productive. This meant that a few people could grow enough food for the entire population, which allowed the population to increase in size. It also freed many people

Although it is not known what the Wagadu army looked like, its troops may have dressed similarly to these soldiers from West Africa.

to follow other occupations besides farming. This allowed Wagadu to maintain large professional armies.

Iron weapons, when placed in the hands of 200,000 soldiers, represented a very powerful opponent. Their efficient spears, fitted with iron points, were far superior to the bone, stone, and wood weapons of their neighbors. Wagadu soldiers equipped with metal swords and spears could easily defeat rivals who fought with wooden rods. The

Wagadu army also included forty thousand archers.

At that time European rulers, such as William the Conqueror, the Duke of Normandy, France, had much smaller armies. William, who successfully invaded England in 1066, controlled only about ten thousand soldiers. William probably did not know that Wagadu existed, but if he had, he probably would not have tried to invade it. His small army would have been crushed by the military might of Wagadu's 200,000 soldiers.

The Wagadu Kingdom absorbed many of the peoples that it conquered. Some of the defeated peoples were allowed to continue living under the authority of their own rulers. But they had to pledge allegiance to the Wagadu kings and pay *tribute*, or taxes, to them.

The kingdom was large. It covered an area about the size of present-day Nigeria. At the height of its power, Wagadu stretched from the Atlantic Ocean in the west to the southern bend of the Niger River in the east. It expanded beyond present-day Mali and Mauritania and into what are now the countries of Senegal and Guinea.

The Wagadu Kingdom stretched to the Atlantic coast of Mauritania, where these fishermen live.

At this time, the only way for a king to communicate with people in other parts of the kingdom was to send a messenger by horseback, which could take many days. This was an inefficient way to run a large country, and it would put any king who ruled from a central capital in a weak position. He could not be in all places at all times to see what was going on and to defend the country's borders. Even if the Wagadu king had appointed local administrators, they would not

Today, as in the past, West African rulers are treated with signs of respect, such as kneeling in their presence.

have been able to react immediately to problems that might arise. Instead, they would have had to wait for their king's decision.

To overcome this difficulty, the Wagadu kings divided ancient Ghana into provinces and appointed princes to rule over them. Although the princes were rulers of their own provinces, they obeyed the central king in Kumbi Saleh and paid taxes to him. This system of government was similar to the European *feudal system*. It gave the king ultimate control over a much larger area than would have been possible if he had ruled alone.

A Wagadu ruler had many roles. In addition to being the military leader, he was also the highest judge and the religious leader of the empire. In fact, the Soninke considered their kings divine, or god-like. Whenever the king appeared, the people fell to the ground and threw dirt on their heads. The Soninke did this as a sign of humility and respect for the divine king, who was believed to represent the spirit or soul of the entire population—past, present, and future.

This combination of roles made the Wagadu king extremely powerful. The Soninke were *matrilineal*, which means that power and identity were passed down through the women of the family. Therefore, when a king died, he was not succeeded by his son, but by his nephew—his sister's son. Although the Wagadu rulers were men, women held very important positions. Matrilineal societies still exist in West Africa.

A POWERFUL TRADE NETWORK

As the Wagadu Kingdom grew and matured, it became more and more powerful. It experienced increasing stability, confidence, and prosperity. The kingdom's power did not, however, come only from its strong military. The stability of the kingdom meant that its people could cultivate its rich and fertile land without fear of war. They grew many crops, such as cotton and the grains millet and sorghum. As these crops prospered, so did the health and wealth of the ancient Soninke people. They had enough food to eat and a surplus of food to sell to others. They began to develop a strong trade network.

Although much of the Western Sudan is dry, it is a fertile region. Grain is stored in granaries such as these.

THE LAND OF GOLD

Trade flourished in Wagadu. But crops were not the only things the Soninke traded. They also traded gold. While early Wagadu kings were called *ghana* because of their military prowess, the title that was used for later kings was *kaya maghan*, which means "master" or "king of the gold." This title is still used by the Soninke people. It refers to another important aspect of Soninke society, the king's power and control over trade, especially trade in gold.

Ancient Ghana's northern boundary was at the edge of the Sahara Desert. It was the perfect resting place for traders who had traveled south across the vast Sahara following the trade routes from Morocco and Mauritania in North Africa and beyond. *Sahel* is an Arabic word for a place to stop or rest before embarking on a long journey. The *sahel* of ancient Ghana attracted many travelers, who wanted to recover after the long journey south across the desert or rest up before leaving on the dangerous trek north across the sands.

The Wagadu Kingdom's southern border lay in the forest region. This region had plants, minerals, and goods different from those available to people living across the desert in North Africa. Merchants and traders from both the north and the south often crossed the large Wagadu Kingdom in order to sell their goods.

Ancient Ghana was therefore surrounded by regions that contained a great variety of resources. The two most important goods traded were salt and gold. Salt is essential to human life, and gold is a luxury desired by many people. Today, because salt is easily available, we tend to forget that salt

A salt plant in Somalia, North Africa. Salt and gold were the two key goods traded in ancient Ghana.

is vital for human survival. To people living in areas without it, salt was worth its weight in gold.

The Wagadu Kingdom was in the perfect position to profit from all of this trade. Its strategic location along the West African trade routes allowed its rulers to become very wealthy and powerful. Northern merchants living in the desert oases who wanted to travel to the southern forests to sell their surplus goods—including salt from Teghaza in the desert, copper, beads, cloth, and books—had to pass through the kingdom. Southern merchants living in

West African jewelry, including three bracelets made from silver (left), ivory (middle), and gold (right). Similar jewelry was probably worn in the Empire of Ghana.

the forest and grasslands who wanted to travel north to sell their gold, ivory, and slaves also had to pass through the kingdom. Other goods were also sold over the years—horses, copper objects, tools, and swords from Arabia, Egypt, and Europe, all of which had to cross ancient Ghana.

TAXES

The kings of Wagadu were able to profit from the transport and sale of these important and expensive goods. They demanded that traders and their cara-

Swords imported from Arabia were important trade items in West Africa.

vans pay a tax each time they entered and left the kingdom. For example, northern traders had to pay one measure of gold to the king for each container of salt they brought into the kingdom, and southern traders had to pay two measures of gold as they carried the same containers out of the kingdom. As a result, traders had to pay taxes twice on the same merchandise: on their way to market to sell and on their way home after buying or trading.

The gold from these taxes went to the Wagadu king. It helped to make him and his kingdom wealthy and powerful. The kings used this money to maintain the Wagadu army and the government, both of which kept the country at peace and trading conditions stable. Without this security, the traders' safety might have been at risk and the trade markets would not have been able to function.

As the kingdom's power and influence grew in the region, it became large enough to be regarded as an empire, the Empire of Ghana.

CONTROLLING THE GOLD TRADE

Many people knew the name of the place where the gold was mined: Wangara. But few people knew where Wangara was, because the trade did not take place at the mines. In fact, foreign traders never met the Wangara traders face-to-face. This protected the gold by keeping secret the location of the gold mines and the identity of the miners. Instead, traders conducted a "silent trade" in which Ghanaian middlemen led foreign traders to a selected site. There the traders unloaded their merchandise (especially salt) onto the ground, beat a large drum to announce their arrival, and left. The Wangara traders then came and placed gold next to the merchandise left by the foreign traders. Then they, too,

Today, as in the past, gold is mined in many parts of West Africa. Gold-bearing soil and water are swirled around in calabashes. This process, called panning, separates light particles of earth from heavy grains of gold.

left. The foreign traders then returned. If they were satisfied that the amount of gold left by the Wangara traders was a fair exchange for the goods that they had brought, they took the gold, beat the drum to mark the end of the trade, and left. If they were not satisfied, they left without taking the gold or beating the drum and waited for the Wangara traders to add more gold (if they agreed to do so).

Just as it is today, gold was a luxury item in Wagadu. The kings carefully controlled the amount of gold leaving the southern mines to ensure that the market never became flooded with gold. The kings knew that if too much gold was available at one time, the gold would lose its value. If gold was common and easy to get, it would no longer be a special object, and its price would fall.

The kings of Wagadu controlled the flow of gold by making rules about who could own it. They kept the gold nuggets for themselves and allowed the merchants to trade only in gold dust. The traders and other people obeyed the kings because they believed that only the king was powerful enough to handle gold nuggets. He could do so because he was divine, but it was thought too

In Wagadu, gold nuggets were kept for the king. Merchants could trade only in gold dust.

dangerous for ordinary people to keep gold nuggets themselves.

The Wagadu kings owned a great amount of gold. Al-Fazari, the first Arabic author to write about ancient Ghana, called it the land of gold. One single gold nugget was rumored to have weighed about thirty pounds. While thirty pounds is not very heavy for a rock, it is for a gold nugget. The price of gold in the 1990s is more than $350 per ounce. That thirty-pound nugget would be worth about $170,000 today. Arab writers also described how one Wagadu king used a large gold nugget as a hitching post

A Berber necklace. Berbers were rivals of the people of ancient Ghana.

for his horse! No wonder visitors were impressed with the kingdom's wealth.

The Wagadu kings made sure that gold's value did not decrease and that the gold supply did not run out. In fact, they continued to control an abundant gold supply long after Europe's gold mines began to run dry. Rulers of other African, European, and Muslim kingdoms had to come to Ghana (or to merchants trading with Ghana and paying taxes to Ghana) for the gold they required to create their own coins and *regalia*.

Ghanaian kings were constantly challenged by their neighbors, who also wished to profit from the gold trade. One of the Soninke people's main rivals was the Sanhaja Berber people, who continually tried to capture some of Wagadu's gold mines. Finally, in about A.D. 990, the Wagadu king took advantage of internal unrest in the Berber city of *Aoudaghast* to the west and captured it. After the rival was defeated, the Wagadu capital of Kumbi Saleh became the main center of trade and knowledge in the Western Sudan region. This was the height of the Empire of Ghana's power.

KUMBI SALEH

Archaeologists, scientists who study how people lived long ago, began excavating the ancient city of Kumbi Saleh only recently, in 1977. Their scientific research has revealed a great deal about the Empire of Ghana and life in the capital. Archaeologists digging in Kumbi Saleh have found, for example, small glass weights that merchants and traders used on their balance scales to weigh their gold. Merchants put the weights on one side of the scale and gold dust on the other. When the two sides balanced, they knew the exact amount of gold they had and its worth.

Archaeological finds are not the only records that

In West Africa, gold merchants still weigh gold dust on scales, as they have done for centuries.

In the last several years, archaeologists have uncovered the foundations of a mosque at Kumbi Saleh, in Mauritania.

tell us about life in the Empire of Ghana. We also know many things about the kingdom from ancient books written by Arab traders and scholars.

ARAB ARMIES

Powerful Arab armies first arrived in North Africa in the seventh century. They had traveled west from the Middle East, south into Egypt, and then all the way across North Africa. They finally reached the West African coast, in present-day Morocco, in about the year 680. The Arab armies conquered all

The deserted town of Ouadane, in Mauritania, gives an idea of what Kumbi Saleh might once have looked like.

the peoples they met along the way. They intended to expand their invasion into Europe by crossing the Strait of Gibraltar and conquering Spain too. But the Moors living in Morocco, whom the Arabs had conquered, told them about a kingdom south of the Sahara Desert that was rich in gold. The Arabs decided to split their army in two and attack both that kingdom and Spain.

The soldiers that went north to invade Spain in about 712 were so successful that they crossed the Pyrenees Mountains and fought their way into what is now southern France. The Arab armies moving south into the fabled land of gold—the empire of Wagadu—were not as successful. They were surprised to find a powerful and organized army defending Wagadu. The Arabs eventually gave up. They settled in North Africa and decided that it was better to trade with Wagadu than to fight its powerful armies.

Soon Arab goods, ideas, *Muslim* religious beliefs, and scholars traveled to the empire of Wagadu. Some of these early scholars wrote about this amazing kingdom. Because the Arabs brought a system of writing with them into Africa, their accounts, written in the Arabic language, are the earliest written descriptions of Wagadu.

DESCRIPTIONS OF THE CAPITAL

Abjullah Abu-Ubaid al-Bakri was an Arab author and geographer who lived in Cordoba, Spain, during the eleventh century. In 1067 he wrote about the Empire of Ghana and its people and customs. Although he did not travel to Wagadu himself, he talked to Arab merchants who did and wrote about what they told him. He also knew a great deal about

Wagadu because Muslims from North Africa had invaded Wagadu thirteen years before, in 1054, and had captured the important trading city of Aoudaghast. Because Cordoba was Muslim-ruled as well, al-Bakri was living in a good place to learn about Aoudaghast and its Soninke inhabitants.

Based on his research and on conversations with eyewitnesses, al-Bakri described Kumbi Saleh as a large city of thirty thousand people. It was famous and attracted many foreign scholars. As was common in Africa, "the city" of Kumbi Saleh was actually two separate cities, located about six miles apart. The Soninke lived in one city, and foreign traders lived in the other. It was probably difficult to see where one city ended and the other began, however, because the suburbs of the two cities lined the road connecting them and blurred the boundary between them.

The city inhabited by foreigners—mostly Muslim merchants and scholars—had large, rectangular stone houses, a northern African influence. Some were two stories high. Many of the houses had small, often triangular-shaped niches set in their walls. The niches may have been used for small decorations or

Kumbi Saleh had narrow streets like those still seen in many West African cities today, such as Jenne, in Mali.

The stone houses at Kumbi Saleh often had triangular niches in the walls. Similar niches can be seen in Ouadane, Mauritania, and in contemporary Soninke architecture.

statues. The houses in this Muslim city, like those in the Soninke city, were built along narrow streets that led to a wide avenue where the outdoor market was located. The foreigners' city also had twelve mosques, where the Muslims worshiped. In fact, the Empire of Ghana became wealthy in part because of its contacts with and acceptance of Muslims, who were the main traders and scholars.

EL-GHABA

The Wagadu emperor lived in the Soninke city, which was also called El-Ghaba. This part of El-Ghaba was described by al-Bakri as a walled fortress. The circular houses were made of clay walls and large, wooden beams that supported thatched, dome-shaped roofs. The homes of wealthy people were made of stone and wood. The largest and most elaborate house was the emperor's palace. It was made up of many small houses with round roofs and was surrounded by a wall. It was not dark like many European castles because it had several windows to allow in light.

The Wagadu emperor held court in this impressive palace, which was luxuriously decorated with paintings, sculptures, and gold. The king himself was splendidly dressed. At the height of the Empire of Ghana's power, he was the only Soninke who was allowed to wear imported and tailored (sewn) clothing. Everyone else living in El-Ghaba wore unsewn cotton, silk, or *brocade* cloth draped around their bodies.

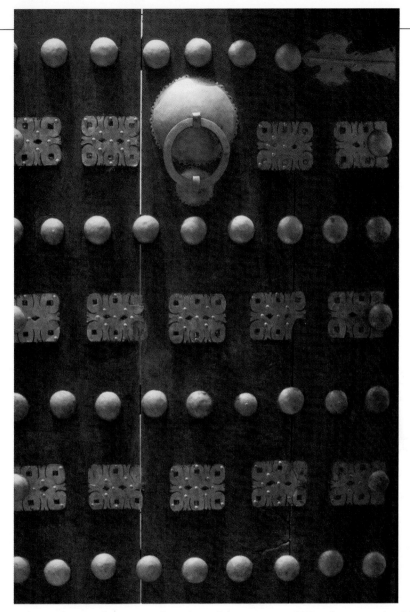

According to historical accounts, the palace of the emperor of Wagadu was a splendid sight. This ornamented door from Timbuktu gives some idea of how the emperor's palace might have been decorated.

4 RELIGION

The name El-Ghaba means "the forest." It referred to a sacred grove of bushes within the Soninke part of the city. The grove contained the royal tombs and statues of past kings. The entire city was considered sacred because it was both the royal center and the spiritual center of the empire.

THE ANCESTORS
The inhabitants of El-Ghaba were not Muslim, and the city had only one mosque, which was built for visiting Muslim dignitaries. In the later years of the Empire of Ghana, increasing numbers of people in the empire converted to Islam, the

Many Soninke were followers not of Islam but of a religion based on their ancestors. In similar African religions, the ancestors are believed to influence the lives of present-day people. These terra-cotta figures are about 750 years old. The scarification marks between some of the figures' eyes and ears are still worn by some Soninke today.

Muslim religion. Many of the emperor's ministers became Muslim. The ruling Soninke people, however, remained primarily non-Muslim. They followed a religion that was based on their ancestors. The ancestors, especially the royal ancestors, were thought to be very powerful. Their power came from their close connections to both the spirit world and the world of the living. They had lived in the world of the living before they died and in the world of the spirits after death. The Soninke people believed that the ancestors could speak the languages of both worlds and that they could speak to the spirits on behalf of their descendants. Therefore, if the living took care of their ancestors, the ancestors would take care of their descendants in return.

THE HOLY SNAKE

The Soninke religion was also based on a great and powerful black snake named Wagadu-Bida. Bida, the holy snake, was believed to live in a cave inside the sacred grove and was the guardian spirit of the royal clan. Because the snake guarded the king's soul, and the king in turn was the divine ruler and protector of the empire and its people, Wagadu-Bida was seen as the guardian of the empire. This is one explanation of why the Soninke people called themselves the people of Wagadu. The other explanation is that the name is related to the word *wago*, which is the name of the Soninke ruling class.

ROYAL TOMBS

Al-Bakri also mentions royal tombs in the sacred grove. He writes that the grove, the snake, and the graves of the ancestral kings were guarded by priests who would not allow anyone into the grove. The kings themselves entered the grove only twice—when they were crowned and when they died. Kings, and perhaps their sisters and mothers, were buried in royal tombs inside the grove. Their graves were large pits under huge, wooden domes. The tombs were provided with everything the kings might want or need in the next life, the life after death. Food, drink, clothing, jewelry, weapons, tools, furniture, and mats were all buried in the tomb with the deceased rulers. Some of each king's servants were also buried with him in the royal tomb. In this way, it was believed, the servants could continue to serve their king throughout eternity.

After a king's body, burial goods, and servants were placed in his grave, it was covered with mats and layers of earth until it became a large, earthen mound. Many mounds were found in Kumbi Saleh when it was excavated. This suggests that Abjullah Abu-Ubaid al-Bakri's descriptions were fairly accurate.

ART

The Empire of Ghana's wealth was often described by writers like al-Bakri. He wrote that the king and members of his court wore elegant gold jewelry and gold clothing. Gold was also used for the royal emblems and ornaments and for drums, shields, and swords. The Wagadu kings used their great wealth to decorate their courts and receiving halls luxuriously. They also kept fine horses and dogs. The animals were sleek and well groomed and they wore collars and ornaments of gold and silver. This extravagant splendor im-pressed visitors and showed them how rich and

Textiles and leather goods were among the many goods sold in the markets of Kumbi Saleh.

Pottery was an important trade item in ancient Ghana.

powerful the Empire of Ghana was.

The Ghanaian emperors were known as the richest rulers in the world. Another Arab writer, Al-Idrisi, who lived in Italy during the 1100s, wrote that Ghanaian emperors hosted the most elaborate banquets ever known. They invited and fed thousands of guests at these fabulous feasts.

The great riches of the Empire of Ghana included many arts and a flourishing culture. Kumbi Saleh's markets were filled with exotic foods, arts, and merchandise from all over Africa and beyond. Among the things for sale were cattle and sheep; dried fruits, such as dates and raisins; Spanish and Moroccan clothing; cowrie shells (used as a type of money in many African cultures); metals; ivory; and pearls. Locally made objects for sale included leather items, pots, metal tools and weapons, gold and copper jewelry, and textiles. All of these goods were paid for with gold dust.

Kumbi Saleh's market was also a source of slaves. Northern merchants bought slaves, whom the Soninke had captured from smaller and weaker neighboring peoples to the south, and took them

Kumbi Saleh was an important Islamic center. Seen here are pages from a seventeenth-century miniature Koran, the holy book of Islam. The Arabic writing is accompanied by decorative symbols that were believed to have magical power.

north where there was a steady demand for them.

Archaeologists digging in the remains of Kumbi Saleh have found a great deal of evidence pointing to the wealth of the empire but little solid gold. They have discovered many pottery fragments, glass counterweights for gold, metal weapons, knives, farming tools, nails, and even some beautiful scissors. They have also found stones painted with verses from the *Koran*, the Islamic holy book that Muslims believe was revealed to the Prophet Muhammad at the beginning of the seventh century. These discoveries tell us that during the Middle Ages—when most of the

Today, as in the past, children in many parts of West Africa study the Koran. Seen here is a Koran class.

people of Europe suffered disease, fear, ignorance, and oppression—the Soninke people of the Empire of Ghana enjoyed a world that was rich in culture and famous as a center of learning.

5 THE FALL OF THE EMPIRE

A legend about Wagadu-Bida—the great black snake that lived in the sacred grove of Kumbi Saleh—explains the fall of the Empire of Ghana.

In the beginning, before the Wagadu Kingdom developed into the mighty Empire of Ghana and before the Soninke's first ancestor, Dinga, arrived, Bida lived in the Western Sudan. After Dinga and his family settled in the region, one of Dinga's sons, named Dyabe, made a deal with the snake. Dyabe agreed that once a year the most beautiful young woman in the society would be sacrificed to Bida. In return, Bida allowed Dyabe and his Soninke descendants to build a great city, which became known as Kumbi Saleh. Kumbi Saleh and the Wagadu empire prospered for many years. But the legend tells us that one year a young warrior loved the young woman who was about to be sacrificed. He loved her so much that he decided to kill Bida to save her life.

The warrior, whose name was Amadou Sefedokote, hid in the sacred grove. When Bida came out of his cave, Amadou cut off its head. The sacred snake was powerful, however. Each time Amadou cut off its head, a new one grew in its place. It was not until the seventh head was cut that the snake finally died. The woman, whose name was Sia, was saved. But because Dyabe's promise had been broken, terrible things began to happen to the Soninke.

Each head that Amadou cut off is said to have flown through the air. The site where each head landed suddenly became rich with gold. This meant that the Soninke no longer had sole control over the gold market, and they lost the power that went with their control.

In addition, after Bida died a terrible drought fell upon the land. The drought lasted seven years.

Drought, which still often affects many parts of West Africa today, may have contributed to the downfall of the Empire of Ghana. The people in this picture are pounding grain.

The farmers' crops died, and the Soninke had little to eat or drink. Many people died. People who were strong enough left the cursed land. Even great cities like Kumbi Saleh were abandoned.

This legend may give us a clue as to what truly brought about the end of the great and powerful

Empire of Ghana. Perhaps a terrible drought did indeed weaken the empire so much that it was easily conquered.

Additional information about why the empire collapsed comes from historical texts. Arab writers tell us that the ancient kingdom of the Soninke fell because of economic and political problems. After the Empire of Ghana reached its greatest power in the eleventh century, competition with many of its neighbors for control of trade eventually weakened its power.

The empire finally fell to the *Almoravids*, a religious group of Berber nomads. Under the leadership of their founder, Ibn Yacin, the Almoravids strictly followed the teachings of the Koran. Although the Wagadu kings had allowed religious freedom within their kingdom—including the Islamic faith—the Almoravids did not tolerate non-Muslim beliefs. They regarded as offensive the Soninke belief in many gods and the belief that the king was divine. These Soninke beliefs violated the rule in the Koran against worshiping gods other than Allah.

The Almoravids decided to conquer the

The spread of Islam in northern and western Africa led to the building of numerous beautiful mosques.

wealthy Empire of Ghana. In 1054 Ibn Yacin's successor, Abu Bakr, led the Almoravid armies and captured the city of Aoudaghast. Then in 1070 they invaded the territory of the original Wagadu Kingdom. The Almoravids finally defeated the empire's armies and conquered Kumbi Saleh in 1076. The Almoravids killed many people and forced the survivors to convert to Islam. Anyone who resisted was killed.

The Almoravids did not remain in control long, however. The proud Ghanaians staged continuous rebellions, and the Almoravids also fought among themselves. Abu Bakr was killed only eleven years after the takeover of Wagadu, after which the Almoravids had to struggle to maintain control. Wagadu armies regained some control, but they were not powerful enough to rebuild the empire. In about 1235, after almost two hundred years of struggle, the region finally fell to the next great empire of the Western Sudan, the Empire of Mali.

The example set by the Empire of Ghana was later followed by the empires of Mali and Songhay. The city of Jenne in present-day Mali became one of several important centers of Islam and trade. Seen here is the famous mosque at Jenne.

6 A LASTING LEGACY

The importance of the Empire of Ghana was not forgotten, however. It had invented a method for creating and running a powerful West African state. Key strategies included controlling the supply of gold, building many trade links, and appointing authorities to rule areas far from the capital. Both the Empire of Mali and, later, the Songhay Empire followed the pattern first used by the Empire of Ghana.

The Empire of Ghana also lives on in another way. In 1957 the British colony of Gold Coast became the first European colony to be returned to African rule. It marked its independence by

This gold ornament was made by the Asante people, who live in the modern country of Ghana.

adopting the new name Ghana in honor of the great achievements of the earlier African empire.

TIMELINE

A.D. c. 250	Ancient Ghana possibly established
c. 570	Birth of the Prophet Muhammad
c. 680	Arabs reach Northwest Africa (Morocco)
c. 712	Arabs invade Spain
c. 750	Ancient Ghana begins to flourish
c. 990	Ancient Ghana captures Aoudaghast
1054	Abu Bakr leads the Almoravid armies to capture Aoudaghast
1066	William the Conqueror invades England
1067	Abjullah Abu-Ubaid al-Bakri, Arab author and geographer who lives in Cordoba Spain, writes about ancient Ghana
1070	Almoravid armies invade Wagadu
1076	Almoravids defeat the Wagadu armies and conquer Kumbi Saleh
c. 1400	Wagadu falls to the Empire of Mali
c. 1450-1600	Empire of Songhay
1914	Ruins of Kumbi Saleh found by archaeologists

GLOSSARY

Almoravids nomadic Muslims, members of an extremely pious religious sect

Aoudaghast important trading city captured by the Ghanaian Kingdom in A.D. 990 and then by the Almoravids in 1054

brocade textile whose decoration is made by "floating" some of the woven threads across the top of the fabric, to create a smooth pattern

clan group of families that have all descended from a single ancestor

feudal system European political system under which the people work for and pay taxes to an overlord, who owns the land on which they work

griot professional oral historian who studies, recounts, and keeps alive a people's history

Koran holy book of Islam

matrilineal system of descent based on female relationships, in which power and identity are passed down through the mother

Muslim one who believes in Islam

regalia objects, symbols, and decorations worn or displayed to symbolize royalty

sahel Arabic word for a place to stop or rest before embarking on a long journey

tribute payments made to a ruler in the form of taxes or goods

FOR FURTHER READING

Chu, Daniel, and Elliott Skinner. *A Glorious Age in Africa.* New York: Zenith Books, 1965.

Davidson, Basil. *Africa in History: Themes and Outlines.* London: Weidenfeld and Nicolson, 1968.

_____. *African Civilizations Revisited.* Trenton, NJ: Africa World Press, 1991.

Fage, J. D. *A History of Africa.* New York: Alfred A. Knopf, 1978.

July, Robert W. *A History of the African People*, 3rd ed. New York: Scribner's Sons, 1980.

Oliver, Roland, and J. D. Fage. *A Short History of Africa.* New York: Facts on File, 1989.

Vlahos, Olivia. *African Beginnings.* New York: Viking Press, 1967.

WEB SITES

Due to the changeable nature of the Internet, sites appear and disappear very quickly. Internet addresses must be entered with capital and lowercase letters exactly as they appear.

Baobab Project: http://web-dubois.fas.harvard.edu/Dubois/Baobab/baobab.html

Connections: http://asu.alasu.edu/academic/advstudies/1b.html

Glimpses of the Kingdom of Ghana in 1067 C.E.: http://www.humanities.ccny.cuny.edu/history/reader/ghana.htm

INDEX

Islam, 40–42, 53,
    55

J
jewelry, 43, 44, 47

K
kaya maghan (king),
    19
kings, divinity of,
    17, 42–43, 53
Koran, 48, 53
Kumbi Saleh, 7, 16,
    29, 30–38, 47,
    50–52, 55

L
language
    Arabic, 12, 34
    Mande, 8, 12
learning, centers of,
    8, 49

M
Mali, 7, 14, 55
matrilineal society,
    17
Mauritania, 7, 14,
    20
middlemen, 24–26
military power, 12
Morocco, 20, 32–33
mounds, burial, 44
Muhammad, 48

O
oral history, 8–10

origin,
    myth of, 8–9
    oral histories
        about, 10–11

P
painting, 38
palace,
    emperor's, 38
provinces, develop-
    ment of, 15–17

R
religion, 40–49
resources,
    natural, 20–21

S
sacrifice, legend of,
    50–52
Sahara Desert, 6,
    20, 33
sahel (resting place),
    20
salt, 20–21
Sanhaja Berber
    people, 29
sculpture, 38
Senegal, 7, 14
"silent trade," 24–25
slaves, 22, 47
snake, holy, 42–43,
    50–52
Songhay Empire, 57
Soninke people,
    8–17, 35, 42,
    50

Spain, 33–34
spirits, 17, 42

T
taxes, 14, 22–24, 29
Teghaza, 21
tombs, royal, 43–44
trade, 18–29, 53
traders, 20, 21–22,
    35–37

W
Wagadu, 12, 14, 18,
    43, 55
Wagadu-Bida, 42,
    50
wago, 11, 43
Wago people, 11–12
Wangara, 6, 24–26
weapons, 12–14,
    22, 43, 47, 48
weights, glass, 30,
    48
West Africa, 6, 10,
    21, 32, 57
Western Sudan, 6,
    8, 29, 50, 55
William the Con-
    queror, 14
women, role of, 17
writers, Arabic, 12,
    27, 32, 34, 43,
    44, 47, 53

ACKNOWLEDGMENTS

The author would like to thank her family, friends, and colleagues for their continued support during this project.

ABOUT THE AUTHOR

An assistant professor at Bowling Green State University, Rebecca L. Green is an Africanist art historian specializing in the art and culture of Madagascar. She earned her B.A. at the University of California Santa Barbara and her M.A. and Ph.D. at Indiana University. Her research has been funded by the Social Science Research Council, Fulbright-Hays, Indiana University Women's Studies and African Studies programs, and the American Association of University Women. She has participated in several national conferences, including the African Studies Association, the Arts Council for the African Studies Association, and the Textile Society of America, and has worked at the Indianapolis Museum of Art.